THE FINAL WEEK

FAMILY EASTER DEVOTIONAL

DAKOTA STEPHENS

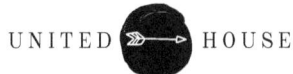

The Final Week —Copyright ©2025 by Dakota Stephens
Published by UNITED HOUSE Publishing

All rights reserved. No portion of this book may be reproduced or shared in any form–electronic, printed, photocopied, recording, or by any information storage and retrieval system, without prior written permission from the publisher. The use of short quotations is permitted.

All Scripture references included are from the English Standard Version (ESV). Unless otherwise notated. It is recommended to read using this translation for the best use of the devotional.

ISBN: 978-1-952840-60-9

UNITED HOUSE Publishing
Waterford, Michigan
info@unitedhousepublishing.com
www.unitedhousepublishing.com

Cover Layout and Interior Design:
Matt Russell, Marketing Image, mrussell@marketing-image.com

Printed in the United States of America
2025—First Edition

SPECIAL SALES
Most UNITED HOUSE books are available at special quantity discounts when purchased in bulk by corporations, organizations, and special-interest groups. For information, please e-mail orders@unitedhousepublishing.com

To the families of Friendship SBC,
I could not have accomplished this writing
without your love and support of me
as your family ministry pastor.

TABLE OF CONTENTS

HOW TO USE THIS DEVOTIONAL 7

Day 1 — PALM SUNDAY. 9

Day 2 — MOPPING MONDAY. 13

Day 3 — TRAPPING TUESDAY. 17

Day 4 — WICKED WEDNESDAY. 21

Day 5 — TABLE THURSDAY. 25

Day 6 — GOOD FRIDAY. 29

Day 7 — SILENT SATURDAY 33

Day 8 — RESURRECTION DAY. 37

ACKNOWLEDGMENTS. 41

NOTES 43

ABOUT THE AUTHOR 45

HOW TO USE THIS DEVOTIONAL

Praise be to God, this devotional landed in the hands of a family eager to learn more about God and His Word. This eight-day devotional will guide you through a deep dive into the final week of Jesus' life, Sunday through Sunday. The different segments presented are what most theologians agree to be day breaks in the text given to us in the Gospel according to Luke. As you read, there are four 'key points' to look for in the text. After the reading, take time with your family to read the questions in the 'engage' section with one another. Try your best to answer them together. If you get stuck, no worries! Go on to the next one until you have read through all four questions. On the next page, there will be a short explanation for each question. Finally, each 'key point' has a designated 'extra reading' verse if you wish to understand the heart of the point further. I pray that as you walk through this devotional with your spouse, children, family members, or even yourself, you will be edified, learn more, and grow closer to our Lord and Savior Jesus Christ.

COUNTOWN: 7 DAYS

PALM SUNDAY

Read:
John 1: 1-15

KEY POINTS

The Colt
The Coming King
The Critics
The Weeping Savior

EXTRA READING

Zechariah 9:9
2 Kings 9:13
Psalm 96
Luke 18:31-34

ENGAGE

1. What is the significance of the colt?

2. What kind of King were the people looking for?

3. Why did the Pharisees criticize the praises of the disciples?

4. Why did Jesus weep?

THE COLT

The colt served as a means to fulfill the prophecy found in Zechariah 9:9. The Jews regarded animals that have never been ridden as suited for holy purposes. Hence why the Lord used the colt, he was going into town to present himself fully as the Messiah.

THE CRITICS

The Pharisees demanded Jesus to silence the praise and singing of His disciples. Yet, just as Psalm 96 says, this is impossible. For all of creation will sing the glorious praise of the marvelous Savior! Philosophy tried to silence the voice of faith. Yet, like trying to suppress a ball underwater, at some point, it will shoot back up again!

THE COMING KING

The people rejoiced when they heard King Jesus coming to town. The disciples were singing His praises. The people were looking for a conquering king, so they threw down their garments (2 Kings 9:13). This was the sign that they accepted Jesus as the King of the Jews.

THE WEEPING SAVIOR

Why did Jesus weep? He knew the same people who now cried out to Him as Lord would soon cry out to crucify the Savior. He also knew of the coming judgment and destruction of the city and its people (Luke 9:21-22; 13:31-35; 18:31-34; 19:41).

COUNTOWN: 6 DAYS

MOPPING MONDAY

Read:
Luke 19:45-48
"Jesus Cleanses the Temple"

KEY POINTS	**EXTRA READING**
The Merchants	John 2:14-16
The House	Isaiah 56:7
The Teacher	Luke 2:41-52
The Destroyers	Luke 18:31-3

ENGAGE

1. What were the merchants doing?

2. Why is the temple called a house of prayer?

3. What do you think Jesus was teaching in the temple?

4. Why do the men want to destroy Jesus?

THE MERCHANTS

This was not the first time that Jesus had driven out merchants from the house of the Lord. In John 2:14-16, Jesus did an extensive cleansing of the temple. This is the second thing John recounts of Jesus doing in his ministry. The merchants were making the temple, the holy place, a den of thieves and robbers. They were using it for self-gain instead of for worship.

THE TEACHER

Jesus' teaching in the temple completes a full circle. Look to Luke 2:41. When Jesus was at the temple for the first time as a boy, He was able to ask questions. The "student" then became the teacher. Instead of Jesus asking questions and showing how great He was at understanding, He was now teaching others about the word of the Lord. Little did they know, the Lord of Hosts was their teacher.

THE HOUSE

The Lord makes it known in Isaiah 56:7 that His house should be called: "a house of prayer." This is what the house of the Lord is designed to be, not a shopping district. It is meant to be a place where God's people can go to Him and talk about their sins, and their woes. Prayer is a central part of ministry for the temple. This is where people experience the presence of the Lord.

THE DESTROYERS

The chief priests and scribes sought to destroy Jesus because Jesus preached salvation through belief in the Son of God. He preached this instead of all the laws that the priests and scribes held in order to be seen as pious, holy, and righteous. This man, who claimed to be God, favored the "sinners" instead of the chief priests who claimed to be holy.

COUNTOWN: 5 DAYS

TRAPPING TUESDAY

Read:
Luke 20:19-26
"Beware the Scribes"

KEY POINTS	**EXTRA READING**
The Spies	Luke 20:1-21:37
The Question	John 2:18-25
The Perceiver	Romans 13:1-7
The Answer	1 Peter 2:13-25

ENGAGE

1. What was the purpose of the spies?

2. What is wrong with the question the spies asked?

3. How was Jesus able to detect the trap?

4. Do you understand Jesus' answer to the question given by the spies?

THE SPIES

How interesting the text says that the spies pretend to be righteous as they stand before the righteous one. But their purpose is to trap Jesus, so they can hand Him over to Pontius Pilate. Look at the picture here: Jesus standing in the open, truly righteous, teaching with His own authority. But the Religious leaders hide behind spies, pretending to be righteous, and have no authority.

THE PERCEIVER

Jesus is able to see that the spies are merely speaking words of flattery and are only pretending to be righteous. One of Jesus' first trips to the temple results in this truth being proclaimed. John 2:24-25 says that Jesus "knew all people and needed no one to bear witness about man, for he Himself knew what was in man." Why? Because he is God!

THE QUESTION

The spies attempt to flatter Jesus. However, they are hoping Jesus says no to paying taxes, a high offense to the Roman government. No matter their motive, the flattering words about Jesus are true but were spoken with ill intent. Furthermore, Jesus has just the right answer to their question.

THE ANSWER

Jesus says it is lawful to pay taxes to governments. Jesus provides two insights into paying taxes and submitting to governments. First, all governments are under God and only have control over what is in this world. In this case, a gold coin with Caesar's picture. Second, what has the image of God on it? People! Thus, all people ought to worship God for He is over all things. Therefore, give praise to God but pay your taxes to the government knowing they are under God's authority.

> COUNTOWN: 4 DAYS

WICKED WEDNESDAY

Read:
Luke 22:1-6
"Judas Set to Betray"

KEY POINTS	**EXTRA READING**
The Seekers	Isaiah 53
The Tempter	Job 1:6-12
The Betrayer	Luke 22:21-22
The Price	Matthew 16:26

ENGAGE

1. Why do the chief priests and the scribes secretly seek to destroy Jesus?

2. "Satan entered Judas," what does this mean?

3. Why did Judas seek out the chief priests?

4. There was a physical price given for the betrayal. What was the spiritual cost?

THE SEEKERS

As we saw on Monday, the scribes and priests could find no wrong in Jesus' teachings. If they were to arrest Jesus in front of the people, they would cause a huge battle. So, they had to arrest Him quietly and secretly. Once they had Jesus before trial, then they could send in liars and deceivers to turn the people against Him and reject Him as king of the people. Isaiah 53 tells us of this coming rejection.

THE BETRAYER

Judas sought out the chief priests because He was influenced by the tempter. He betrayed Jesus because he was being deceived and fed lies from the tempter, the deceiver himself, Satan. Judas never truly loved Jesus; he wanted much by doing little. Judas betrayed the Lord of Lords and God had ordained that very appointment.

THE TEMPTER

I imagine Luke 22:3, "Then Satan entered into Judas called Iscariot, who was of the number of twelve," happening much like Job 1:6-12. Satan came before God seeking to destroy another one of His servants. God pointed Satan to Judas, to take over and betray Jesus. Picture the joy Satan had when he heard he would get to help lead Jesus to destruction, to kill the Son of God. Yet, Satan must not have known no person, thing, or authority in heaven or on earth can overcome the mighty King Jesus!

THE PRICE

Jesus asks in Luke 9, what profits a man, to gain the whole world and lose his soul? This is the question we must ask ourselves today. Judas sold his life for the world and the culture. He turned his back on Jesus for 30 pieces of silver. Yet, the spiritual price? He bought his way to hell; he rejected the Savior of the world.

> COUNTOWN: 3 DAYS

TABLE THURSDAY

Read:
Luke 22:7-23
"The Last Supper"

KEY POINTS	**EXTRA READING**
The Passover	Exodus 12:1-28
The Upper Room	Matthew 26:17-29
The Bread	Mark 14:12-25
The Cup	1 Corinthians 11:17-26

ENGAGE

1. What is the Passover?

2. If there were no phones, how did Jesus know about the man who provided the upper room?

3. What does the bread symbolize?

4. What does the cup symbolize?

THE PASSOVER

The feast of Passover or Unleavened Bread was instituted as a reminder to the Jewish people of the exodus from Egypt. Before the last plague in Egypt, the killing of the firstborn, God commanded Israel to paint their doorways with the blood of an unblemished lamb. When the Spirit of God saw the blood of the lamb on a doorway, the Spirit would pass over the house and spare the firstborn. The blood of the lamb satisfied God's wrath.

THE BREAD

The bread represents the body of Jesus Christ. His body was broken in the sense that in His body He suffered the punishment due us. He gave us His body, meaning He died for us in the flesh. Jesus' body truly felt the pain of the cross and the wrath of God. Upon His body, He carried our sins and paid for them in full. Thus, He suffered and died the death we should have, but praise be to God, that Christ died for us!

THE UPPER ROOM

Jesus does not need Expedia, TripAdvisor, or a travel agent, for He is God! Jesus knew exactly what room would be open because Jesus is God. Jesus knows everything and Him knowing about this room demonstrates just that!

THE CUP

After they had finished eating the Passover meal, Jesus took the final cup of wine and declared it to be the blood of the new covenant, His blood.

Jesus' death cleanses us of our sin debt and enters us into a new relationship with God bought with Christ's blood. Jesus' blood is greater than the Passover lamb's blood. For He is the true Passover lamb who died once and for all to save a people for His possession.

> COUNTOWN: 2 DAYS

GOOD FRIDAY

Read:
Luke 23:32-43
"The Crucifixion"

KEY POINTS	**EXTRA READING**
The Skull	Leviticus 16:20-22
The Mockers	Isaiah 53
The Repenter	Romans 10:9-10
The Savior	Romans 6:23

ENGAGE

1. What's important about the place, "The Skull"?

2. Why did the people mock Jesus?

3. What does the one thief realize that the other one does not?

4. How does Jesus respond to the one thief?

THE SKULL

This is the true significance of Golgotha (the skull). Jesus Christ, the Word made flesh, was exiled outside the camp, so that we, who once were far off, could be brought near to Him (Eph. 2:13; Heb. 10:22). He was cut off from the land of the living so we might have life in His name (Isa. 53:8; John 20:31). "Therefore let us go to him outside the camp and bear the reproach that he endured"[1] (Heb. 13:13).

THE REPENTER

One thief realizes who truly is on that cross. He cries out to Jesus to remember him when He goes on to paradise. This shows us that truly salvation is as easy as Christ has instructed it to be: Confess Him as Lord and Savior and you will be saved. The thief on the cross realizes that the man in front of him was the Savior of the world. He wants to be in paradise with the man who was staying on the cross for him.

THE MOCKERS

They mocked Christ for staying on the cross. They shouted, "If you are truly the King of the Jews, save yourself"(Luke 23:37). Yet, it is for us, for God's elected people that Christ stayed on that cross. If Christ were to come off the cross, the cross would have been meaningless, the sacrifice incomplete. It is in faithful obedience and love for the people of God that Christ remained on the cross. For me and you, Christ bore the wrath we are due, so we no longer have to face it.

THE SAVIOR

"Truly I say to you, today you will be with me in paradise"(Luke 23:43). Christ granted the thief salvation, even as He was near death hanging on the cross. All sins, all transgressions, and all debts from the thief were now nailed to the cross with Jesus. They had been forgiven and forgotten. He was made holy, as Christ is holy.

> COUNTOWN: 1 DAY

SILENT SATURDAY

Read:
John 16:19-24 & 33
"A Day of Sorrow"

KEY POINTS

The Departing Jesus

The World's Moment

The Coming Joy

The Coming Victory

EXTRA READING

John 16:25-33

John 14:1-14

Isaiah 53:3

Luke 23:44-56

ENGAGE

1. Put yourself in the disciples' shoes. How sorrowful do you think they were on Saturday?

2. Why does the world rejoice at the death of Jesus?

3. How does Jesus turn sorrow into joy?

4. How does Jesus overcome the world? What does that mean for us?

THE DEPARTING JESUS

The gospels do not detail the day we have coined Silent Saturday. Why would they? It is called Silent Saturday for a reason. However, this passage gives us insight into what the disciples felt. Jesus tells the disciples that in "a little while" they will not see Him. This will result in deep sorrow. Their Lord, Messiah, and friend had just died. Of course, they feel sorrow.

THE COMING JOY

The world has its moment, but in the resurrection the next day, the disciples would no longer have sorrow but joy! Because He lives, the disciples no longer had to suffer in sorrow. Sorrow is not just erased but replaced by joy. As we approach Sunday, let us rejoice as well for Christ is alive! No matter what sorrow we have in this world, we have full joy in Jesus.

THE WORLD'S MOMENT

To make matters worse, not only would the disciples be sorrowful, but the world would be rejoicing. The disciples feel as if all has been lost for they did not understand Jesus would rise again. The world did not know Jesus would rise again either, so they thought they had won. This arrogance has continued even after Jesus' ascension, but their rejoicing is in ignorance. For those in Christ have true joy and victory.

THE COMING VICTORY

John 16:33 says, "You will have suffering in this world. Be courageous! I have conquered the world!" Jesus has conquered the world through his death and resurrection. Although the disciples feel defeated now, victory is on the horizon and is displayed in an empty tomb. Today we stand in the victory of Jesus and can face anything. So be courageous!

RESURRECTION DAY!

RESURRECTION DAY

Read:
Luke 24:1-12
"The Resurrection"

KEY POINTS

The Stone

The Messengers

The Doubters

The Marveller

CONTEMPLATION

Have you professed Jesus as Lord and Savior?

Do you have questions about salvation?

Go and talk to your Pastor!

ENGAGE

1. What is so bizarre about the stone being rolled away?

2. Who are the men beside the empty tomb?

3. Why did the apostles and friends doubt?

4. Why was Peter quick to run to the tomb?

THE STONE

The stone being rolled away was a miraculous feat. The assumption is there were several men needed to close the tomb. Mark 16:3 says that the three ladies who appeared asked, "Who would roll the stone away?" Showing us that this stone was heavy. So, when the men arrived and it was already rolled away, that was a scary sight!

THE DOUBTERS

The disciples doubted because of a historical and cultural tradition ingrained in them to not take women at their word. Culturally, the testimony of women was not admissible by law. However, how great is our God to completely dispel this logic and reveal first to the women that He had risen? The disciples doubted because the mystery of Christ was just that, a mystery. It was not until Christ revealed Himself that the word itself became apparent and known fully by the disciples.

THE MESSENGERS

Luke tells us that there were two men in dazzling apparel next to the tomb. These men are what we consider messengers or angels. The angels were there to instruct the women on how to proceed with the news they had just witnessed. They were to go and tell the disciples that Christ had risen and was no longer in the tomb!

THE MARVELLER

We see in Luke that Peter believed. It's almost as if he had to since he denied Jesus three times a couple of days prior. He marveled at what the Lord had done. He ran to the tomb, wanting to see for himself that the testimony was true. He went home with his sorrow turned to joy!

ACKNOWLEDGMENTS

I would like to express my deepest gratitude to the following individuals, whose unwavering support and encouragement have played an integral role in the creation of this devotional:

My Beloved Wife, Holly:

Your love, patience, and understanding have been my constant inspiration. Thank you for standing by me, offering endless support, and being a constant reminder of Christ's love.

Mentor Extraordinaire, Jesse:

To Jesse, whose guidance and wisdom have been the guiding light of this endeavor. Your mentorship has shaped not only this devotional but also my growth as a writer and pastor.

True Friend, Avery:

Avery, your friendship is a treasure. Your unwavering belief in me and your honest feedback has been invaluable. Thank you for being a constant source of inspiration and laughter.

To all those whose names are not mentioned but have contributed in ways big and small, I extend my heartfelt thanks. This devotional is as much yours as it is mine.

With sincere appreciation,

Pastor Dakota Stephens

NOTES

1. Rosenthal, Shane. 2023. "Where Was Jesus Crucified? - by Shane Rosenthal." The Humble Skeptic. https://shanerose.substack.com/p/where-was-jesus-crucified.

ABOUT THE AUTHOR

Dakota Stephens is a Southern Baptist pastor passionate about proclaiming God's Word and equipping others for discipleship. He serves as the family ministry pastor at Friendship Southern Baptist Church in North Carolina. There he partners with parents to train up children in the way of the Lord. In addition to his pastoral ministry, he enjoys writing, podcasting with fellow Reformed Baptist pastors, and hosting creative events that build up the community. When he's not serving the church, Pastor Dakota is a dedicated husband to his beautiful wife Holly, and father to his two son's Hank and Teddy. He currently attends full time at Judson College, the extension of Southeastern Baptist Theological Seminary. He is currently set to graduate with his B.A in Pastoral Ministry in 2026. He resides in Albemarle, NC and seeks to savor the blessings of family life with every moment the Lord grants him.

www.ingramcontent.com/pod-product-compliance
Lightning Source LLC
Chambersburg PA
CBHW052127070526
44586CB00016B/2117